code
a drone using blocks

1ST EDITION

Ryan Jones
github.com/drjonesy

Acknowledgments

I want to thank the following people for introducing me to aerial drones and development into unmanned systems. To Dr. James Burns for introducing ENVI (the Electric and Networked Vehicle Institute) to those of us attending Coleman University back in May 2015. To Rod Weiss for introducing me to Dr. Burns and Dr. Burn's vision of electric vehicle development and unmanned systems. To Robert Gubala who introduced me to quad-copter development and drone flying. Because of Robert I kept on the path of slowly learning more and more about drone development until it lead me into the tools I will be covering in this book's lessons. To Dan Wolfson who introduced me to the Robolink CoDrone which gave me the desire to find a more simplified solution for non-coders to learn how to control a drone with a code-like environment. To Norma Carter, my Aunt, who was willing to run a test of this course for her 4th and 5th grade parent orientation night in the Poway, CA school district. To Charlie Morgan for effectively teaching me how to program. Finally, to Mike Lebo for his unquenchable thirst for learning drones and desire to show that even an old dog can learn new tricks.

-- Ryan Jones

© Copyrighted ™Trademarked Material

Additional Resources

The most recent course content can be found online at:

https://github.com/drjonesy/ParrotDrone_Airborne_CodingWithTynker

If you prefer to watch a lesson instead of reading, all lessons are provided in video format on YouTube. Just go to the link above, scroll-down to click on the lesson you want, and then click on the video link at the top of the lesson.

Table of Contents

Tools

Before we get into the required Tools needed, it is important that you can read English and have a basic understanding of numbers. There are three required tools: A tablet, the free tynker application, and an approved programmable drone. To succeed in the course you need to be hands on.

Devices

At the time this was published, the only way you can code a drone is with a Tablet. Sadly, a phone won't work. You can use either an Android or iOS tablet. Your table must also be bluetooth enabled!

Examples of these look like the following....

Android Device

Apple iPad

Required App

The app you will use to code the drone in this book is the Tynker App. There are other apps available that offer similar functionality like Tickle, but we will be using Tynker. The App is available in both the iOS App Store for Apple devices and Google Play Store for Android devices.

In the Google play store search for **Tynker**

When you see the results, there might be two options. Choose the Red Icon that is FREE. The name of the app is
Tynker - Learn to code

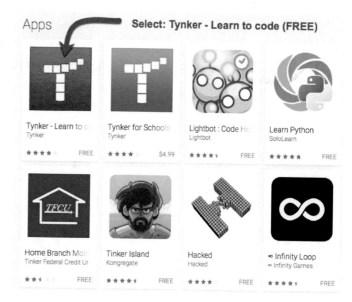

Apple iPad users

Use the app store to search for **Tynker**. Just like the Android users, you will see two results; both a Free and Paid edition. Download the FREE Red edition.
Tynker - Learn to code

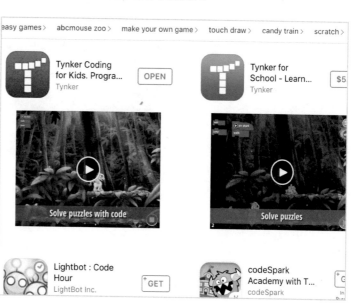

Approved Drones

At the time this was published, the only aerial Parrot drones available for coding with the Tynker App were the Mambo, Airborne Cargo, Airborne Night, Rolling Spider, and Swing.

!!! Important !!! - Certain Drones have propeller shields (frame attachments) around them that can be detached.

The **MAMBO** comes with premier functionality over most of the mini-drones. It includes a tiny pellet shooter and grabber claws. The newest edition on the market has the option to attach an FPV (First Person View) camera to enable it for FPV racing.

The **AIRBORNE CARGO** is available in two colors: white and yellow. The white drone is the Mars edition; whereas, the yellow is the Travis edition. These two drones come with a Lego brick attachment on their backs so you can attach Legos and carry them around like cargo.

MARS

Travis

The **AIRBORNE NIGHT** looks almost exactly identical to the Airborne Cargo drones and it is except for two changes. The Night Drone does not come with a Lego attachment on its back. Instead, it comes with headlights that can be turned on / off, dimmed, flickered, and slow flashing. At full strength these tiny beams of light are blinding!

The night drone comes in three body styles: Maclane, Blaze, and S.W.A.T.

MACLANE

BLAZE

S.W.A.T

The **ROLLING SPIDER** body looks similar to all the Airborne Drones. The key difference in this drone is the plastic wheels that can be attached to it. If you want a drone that can also act as ground vehicle then this might be a good choice.

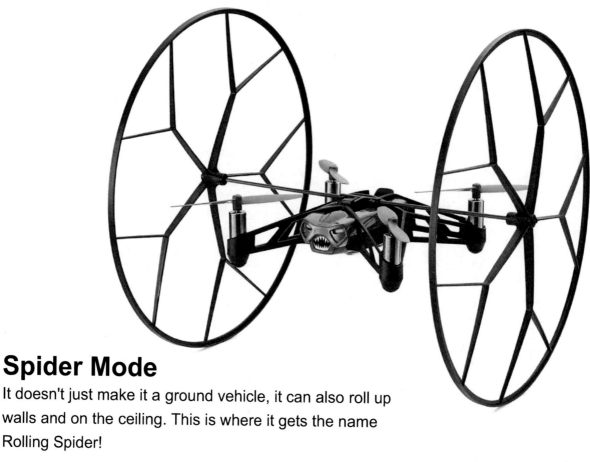

Spider Mode

It doesn't just make it a ground vehicle, it can also roll up walls and on the ceiling. This is where it gets the name Rolling Spider!

Standard Drone Mode

The **SWING** is a bit different than most of the mini-drones. It is both a quad-copter and plane. It starts off as a quad-copter and can stay in that mode or it can rotate 30°, 60°, or 90° (degrees) into plane mode where the speed picks up to 18 mph. Be wary of flying this in plane mode indoors unless you have a lot of space.

Quad-Copter Mode

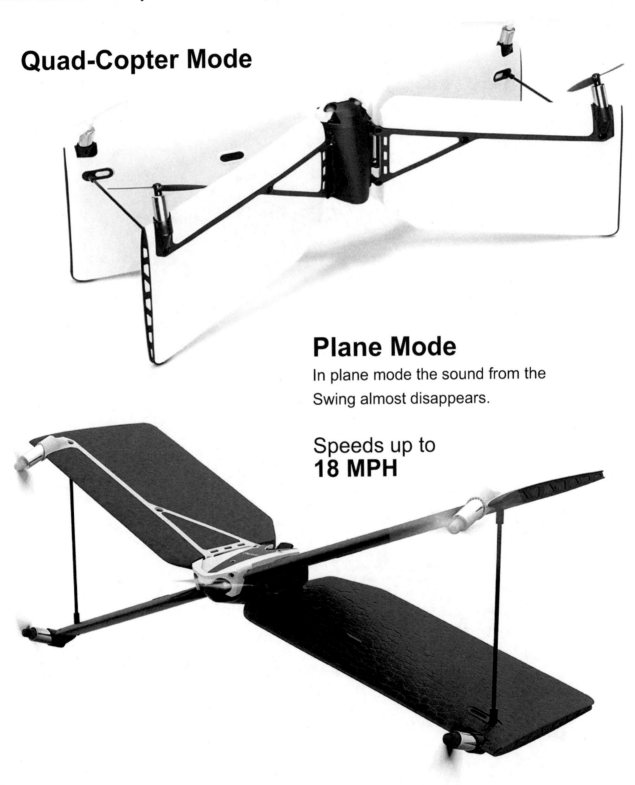

Plane Mode

In plane mode the sound from the Swing almost disappears.

Speeds up to
18 MPH

Setup
How to Create a New Project (Tynker App)

1) Load up the Tynker App on your Tablet

2) Click the **Projects** button

3) Click the **+ box** to Create a New Project

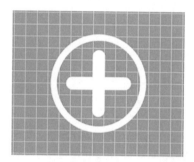

4) Select the **Blank Template** box. It's the one with outlined empty boxes.

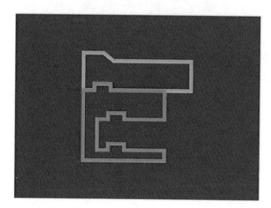

How to Remove an Actor (Tynker App)

1) Touch the Actor and make him active.
If it is active, a white box will show around the actor and three options will be displayed.

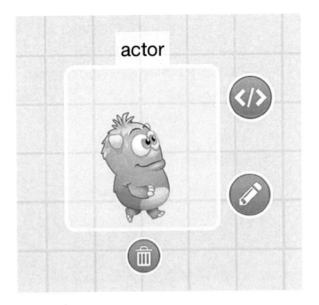

2) Click on the **Trashcan** icon

3) A pop-up window will appear. It will ask you,

   Are you sure you wish to remove "actor"?

4) Click on the **Yes** button

5) The actor will then be removed from the stage

How to add a Drone/Robot (Tynker App)

You should be on the stage. The stage is the area where you just removed the actor.

1) In the top-right of the stage. Find the **plus icon** and click it.

2) A pop-up window will appear to **Add an Actor**.
Select **Connect Device**

3) Another pop-up will appear: **Select an Asset.** Select the drone you are using.
   For this example I will select the yellow cargo drone.

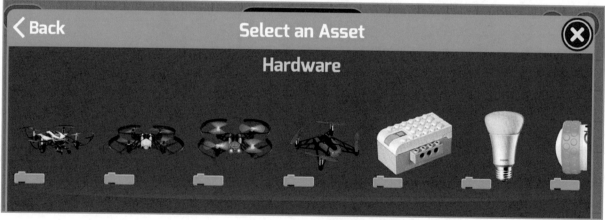

4) You should now see the drone you selected
on the stage. It should be highlighted with the
three options available.

How to connect the Drone to Bluetooth

1) Before connecting the drone to bluetooth you must make sure the battery is properly inserted into the drone. Make sure the clip and bumps are face up. Take at look at the following images for a better understanding. The Battery must be pushed in all the way. It should make a slight snap or clipping sound when it is fully inserted.

Slide in this way

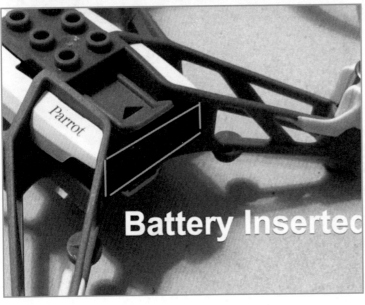

Battery Inserted

Blinking Green Eyes means it is ready for pairing with a bluetooth tablet

2) Once the battery is in, check the front of the drone for flashing eyes. The eyes will flash a light orange/yellow and then begin blinking green. This means the drone is ready to pair with your bluetooth device (tablet).

3) Next make sure your bluetooth is enabled on your bluetooth tablet. Android and iOS are different. I will go over both now.

iOS devices are simple. Take your finger and slide up from the bottom of the tablet's screen. A menu will will appear with icons. The icons that are colored blue are enabled. If your Bluetooth icon isn't blue, then tap it to enable bluetooth.

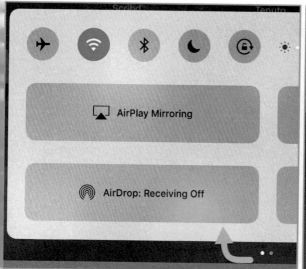 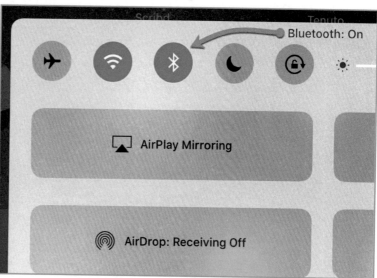

bluetooth OFF   iOS 11   **bluetooth ON**

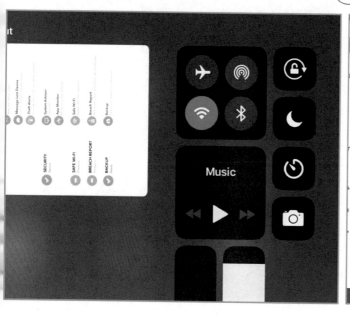 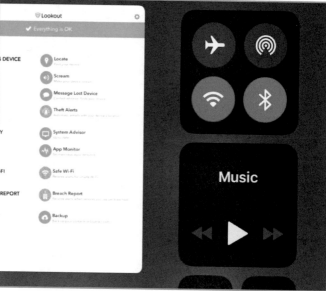

4) Android devices are a little more challenging, because it depends on the device. Some Android devices let you take your finger from the top of the screen and pull down a menu. In this menu you would see the bluetooth icon. -- Clicking on this icon would enable/disable bluetooth or take you to the bluetooth setting where you would enable/disable it.

Follow along with the pictures if you don't know how to enable Bluetooth on Android.

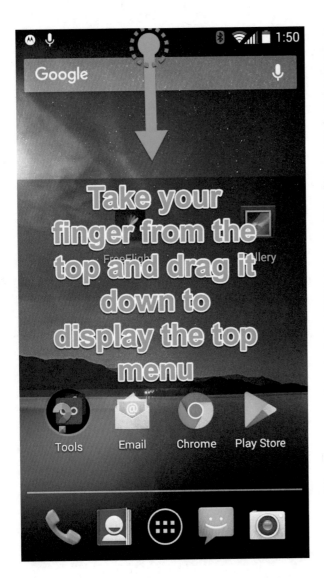 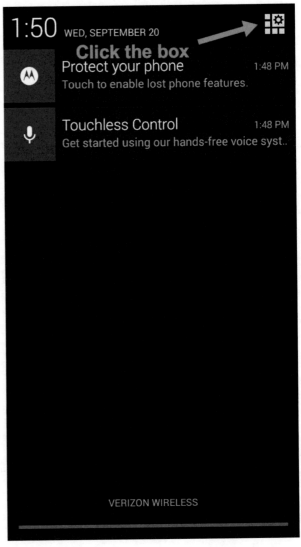

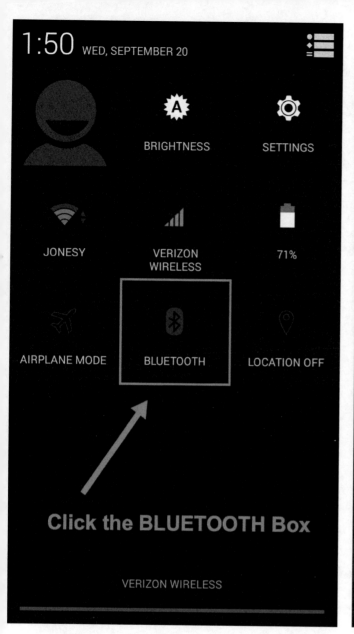

Bluetooth is now enabled. If you do not have the option to pull-down the top menu, try it from the bottom. If that still doesn't work, then you will have to access the bluetooth setting the old-fashioned way.

On the next page you can see the old-fashioned option!

5) The **Old-Fashioned Option** for Android. You only need to do this option if the other Bluetooth enable functionality wasn't available.

Follow the images and the text on each image.

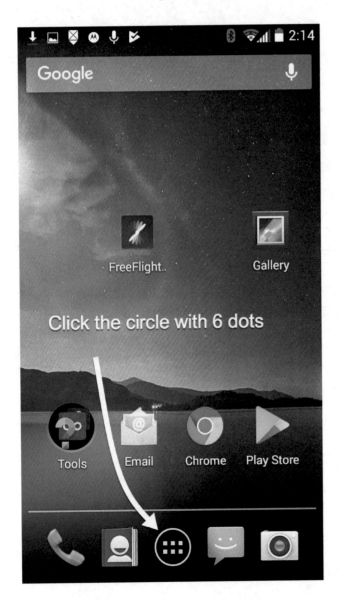

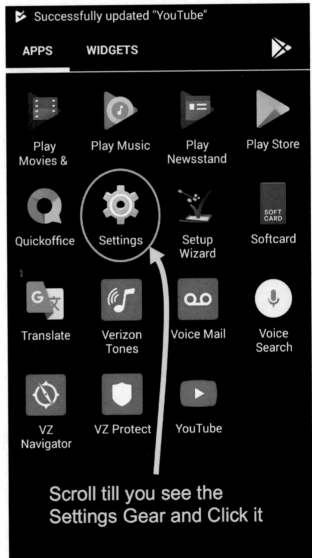

If Bluetooth is OFF tap the OFF button to turn it ON

6) The Drone is powered on and your tablet is bluetooth ready. Jump back into Tynker.

7) On the stage of your current project, you should see your drone. Tap it to make it active if it isn't already active.

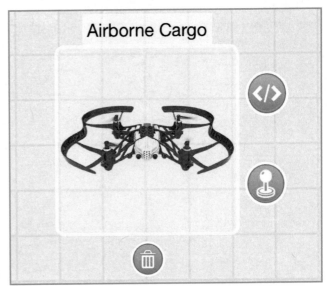

Airborne Cargo

8) With your Drone Actor active, you should see three buttons around the drone. The 1st is the code view, the 2nd is the controller view, and the 3rd is the trashcan (remove actor) button.

9) Click on the Controller Joy Stick Icon. This is the only time we will be using the controller stick. We just want to make sure the drone can connect before we begin building our code.

 Joy Stick Icon

10) On the next screen, you will see the option to control your drone. What we are looking for is the gray block with text that says the name of our drone. In my case the drone name is **Mars_091866**. We want this to show up green. This means it has connected

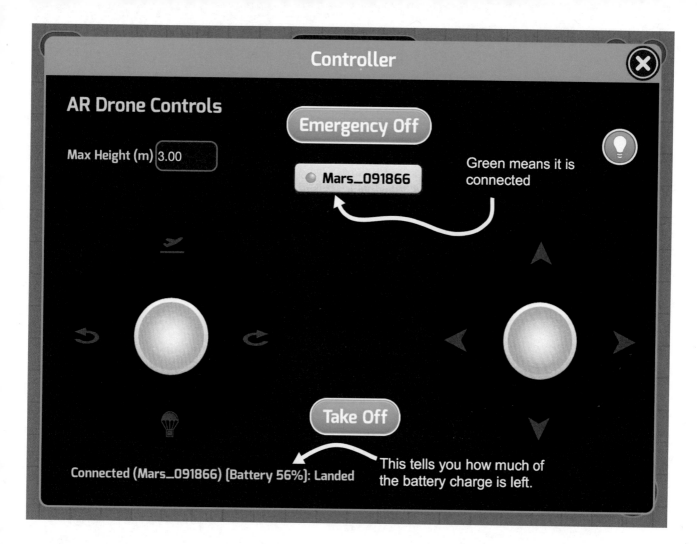

Controller

AR Drone Controls

Emergency Off

Max Height (m) 3.00

○ Mars_091866

Green means it is connected

Take Off

Connected (Mars_091866) (Battery 56%): Landed

This tells you how much of the battery charge is left.

11) The picture above is a screenshot of the Controller View in Tynker on the iPad.

12) Once your drone's name appears and shows a green dot next to it, go ahead and click the **X button** in the top right to close the window.

> *If you are having trouble, make sure that the drone is directly next to the tablet so it doesn't try and connect to another drone.*

13) Congratulations, you've successfully connected your drone to your device.

Important Note...
You will not need to come back to the Controller window again. We only came here to make sure the drone would connect to your tablet. When we get into the code view there is another way to connect to the drone.

Required for All New Drone Projects

It's finally time. We are going begin using the code blocks, but before we add any custom code to our drone project we must first remove the initial set of code blocks.

1) Click on the Drone in Tynker on the
   Stage to make it active.

2) Then click on the **Code Button < / >**

3) Every time we start a new
Blank project we are given starter code.
Sadly, the starter code we are given
doesn't apply to our Aerial Drones,
so we have to get rid of the entire block.

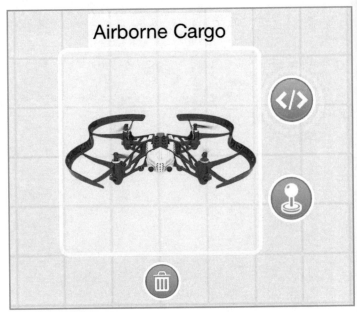

Drag Entire block
over to the left side

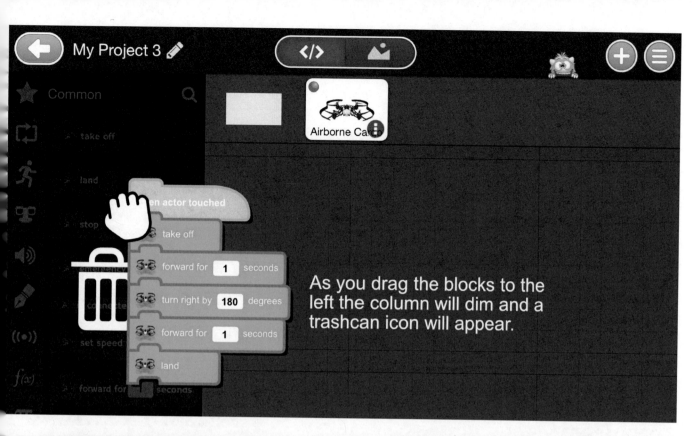

As you drag the blocks to the left the column will dim and a trashcan icon will appear.

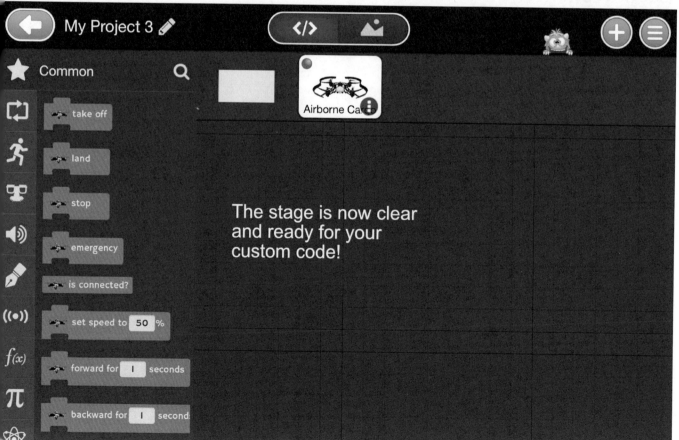

The stage is now clear and ready for your custom code!

Lesson 1: Testing the Drone

For the first lesson we will simply tell the drone to take off and then land.

1) On the left side of the stage are the different blocks we will be using provided by Tynker and Parrot.

2) Notice there are icons to the far left. These are the block categories. Most of our project will only use 5 of the categories. The five include: **Common, Control/Flow, Functions, Math,** and **Library.**

3) Sometimes I will refer to the **Control/Flow** as **Loops**

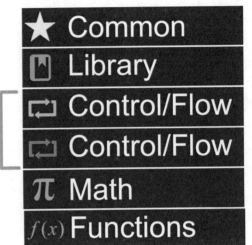

Let's Begin

4) Select either the **Common** or **Control/Flow (Loops)** category

5) Find the **on start** block. Drag it onto the stage

6) Select either the **Common** or **Library** category

7) Find the **take off** block. Drag it onto the stage and under the **on start** block. It will snap together if you are close enough.

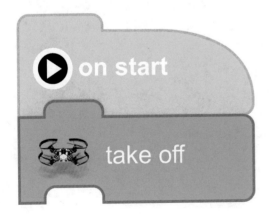

8) Select either the **Common** or **Library** category.

9) Find the **land** block. Drag it onto the stage and under the **take off** block.

10) Click the orange and white play button. If the drone isn't flying, you might need to tap the drone box. It is highlighted in red below. Once the drone has connected, you will see a green dot in the box. It is connected. Push the play button again.

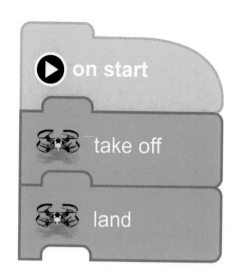

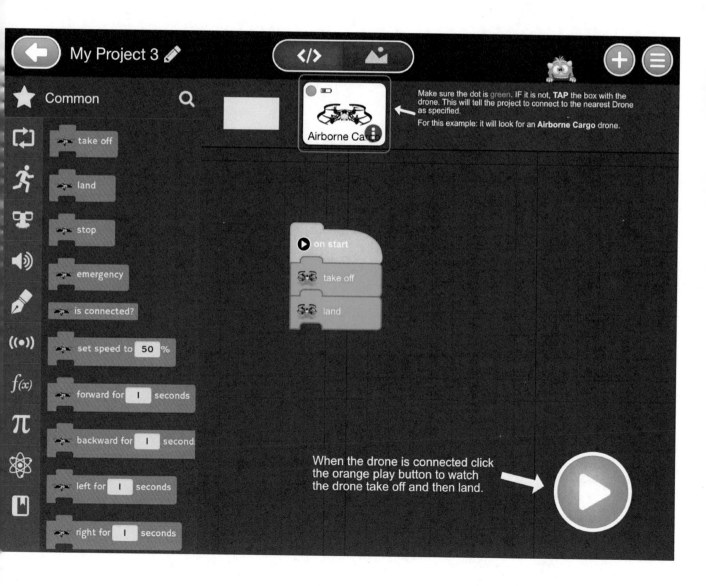

Lesson 1
Challenges

The challenge area is optional but encouraged. Each lesson will be followed by at least one challenge. The challenges will cover the current and all previous lessons.

Challenge 1: Adding a new block

1) Recreate Lesson 1. Add the **on start, take off,** and **land** blocks

2) In the Library category find the **stop** block.

3) Drag it onto the stage and put it between the **on start** and **take off** blocks.

4) Press the orange and white play button.

Think about it?

What did the stop button do? If you are with other people, talk about what you think the stop button does.

Challenge 2: Take off, land, pause, repeat

1) Just like challenge 1, recreate lesson 1 using the **on start, take off,** and **land** blocks.

2) Again, find the **stop** block in the **Library** category.

3) However, place the **stop** block after **land**.

4) You should now have 4 blocks on the screen.

5) After the **stop** block repeat the last three blocks 2 more times

6) Press the **play** button. At this point your should have 10 blocks including the **on start** block on the screen.

Think about it?

What will the drone do now? How does the stop block affect repeat action?

Challenge 3: Create your own combination

For this challenge, you must start with the **on start** block. Use the three blocks **take off, land,** and **stop**. Create your own code and share it if you are in a group or class. Get used to how all the blocks work.

Lesson 2: Block Help

Now that you've created your first project and possibly tackled the challenges in Lesson 1. You might begin to play with more blocks or perhaps you'd like to know what each block does.

There are two ways to finding this information out.

1) In the Tynker Application on the Stage. Find the little monster in the top right he looks like this...

If you need help, drag code blocks over me.

2) Next, drag a block from the stage or the left-side category onto the monster and drop the block onto the monster.

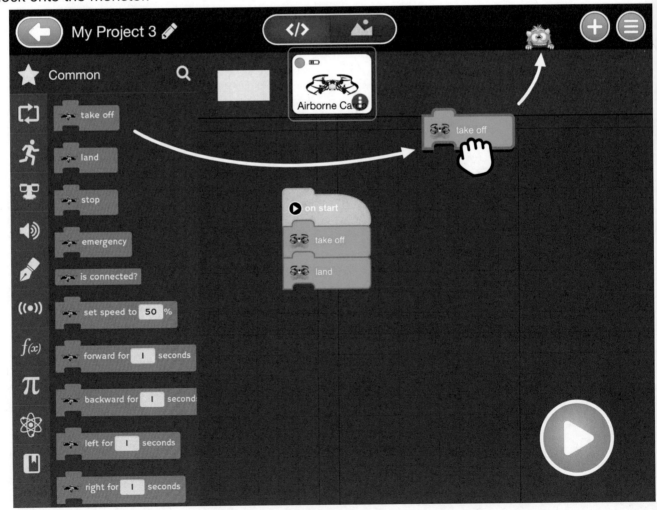

3) After you drop the block, a pop-up window appears explaining what that block can do and how it interacts with other blocks. There might even be an example of how the block can be used. *It might not be obvious, but you can scroll-down in the pop-up window.*

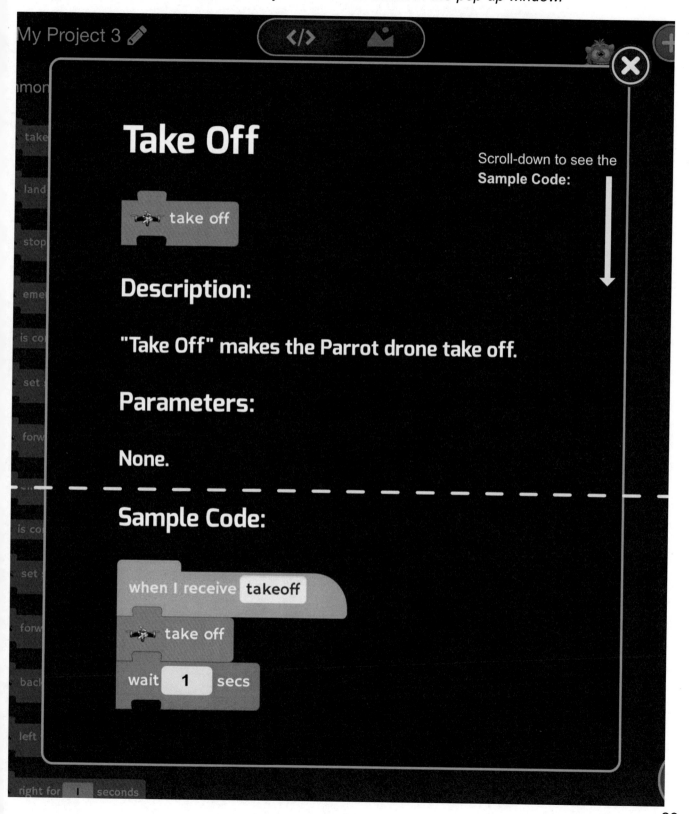

My Project 3

Take Off

Scroll-down to see the **Sample Code:**

take off

Description:

"Take Off" makes the Parrot drone take off.

Parameters:

None.

Sample Code:

when I receive **takeoff**

take off

wait **1** secs

Lesson 2
Challenges

Challenge 1: Land Block

1) Drag the **land** block over the little monster to find out what it does

2) Read the description. What does it say?

Think about it?

Look at the sample code. This is different from what we have done so far. Think about how you might use this sample. Notice the top block in the sample code doesn't have a top-snap block.

Challenge 2: Drag multiple blocks

1) This time, drag all the blocks on the stage onto the monster.

Think about it?

What happens? Does it show an explanation for each block? Why do you think it displays the information it does?

Lesson 3: Flying Forward and Saving

Before we begin, It is important to remember that most lessons will begin with both an **on start** and **take off** block and end with a land block.

Book Terminology: **Create a New Project**
- *When you see the words "Create a New Project" do the following commands.*
[1] Create a New Blank Project in Tynker.
[2] Remove the Actor (monster).
[3] Add an Actor (Connect Device).
[4] Select the Drone you are using.
[5] Click on the Drone to make active.
[6] Select the (< / >) code block.
[7] Remove the start up code.

1) Create a New Project

2) In the **Control/Flow (Loops)** drag an **on start** block onto the stage.

3) In the **Library** drag and snap a **take off** block under the **on start** block.

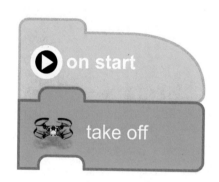

4) In the **Library** find the **forward for [1] seconds** block. If you want to know more about this block, drag it onto the **help monster** in the top-right corner.

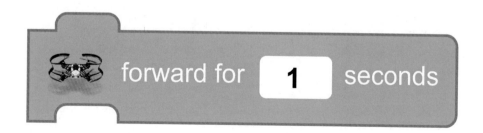

Block Description:
"Forward For" moves the Parrot drone forward for the specified number of seconds.

5) Drag and snap the **forward for [1] seconds** block under the **take off** block.

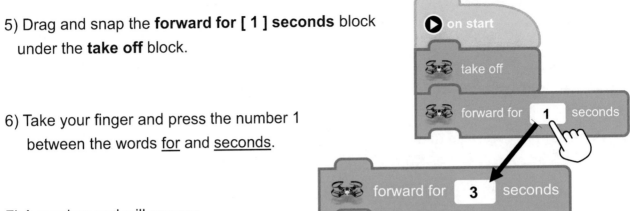

6) Take your finger and press the number 1 between the words <u>for</u> and <u>seconds</u>.

7) A number pad will appear.

Change the number **1** to a **3** and click the **OK** button.

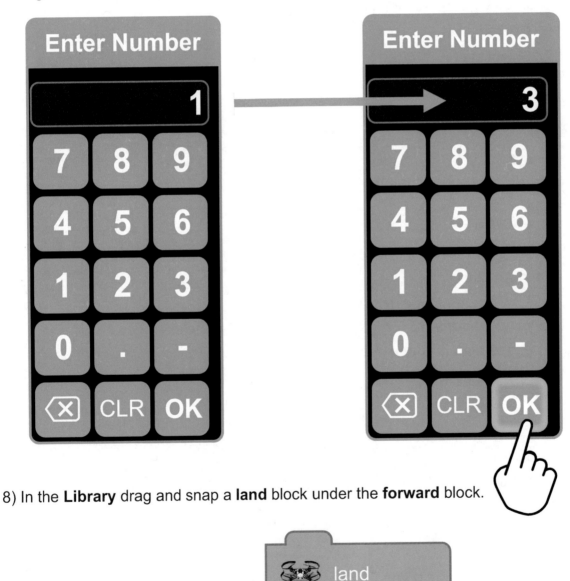

8) In the **Library** drag and snap a **land** block under the **forward** block.

Next we will save the project.

9) Find the **back** arrow in the top-left of the screen. Click it to display the save settings.

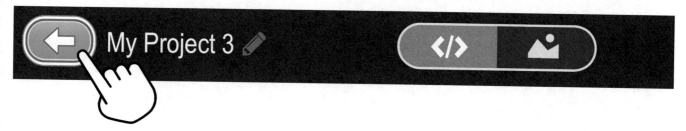

10) Click on the text field to change the project name.
    You might have to backspace to clear the current project title.

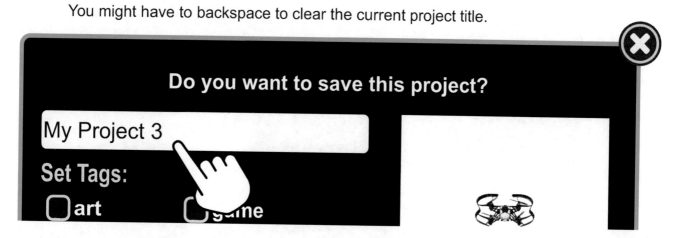

11) Name the project **Fly Forward and Save** (save is part of the name)
12) Click **Done** for iOS and the **return arrow** for Android

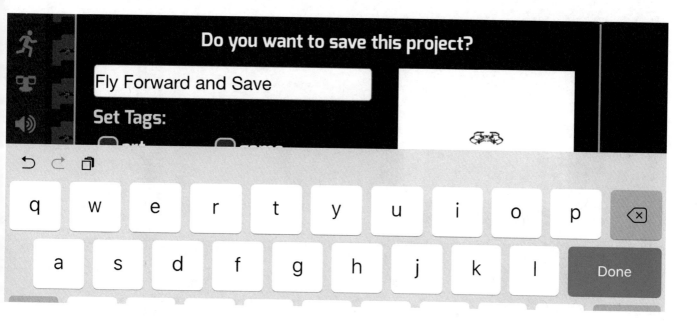

13) Check **learn** and **robotics** under Set Tags.

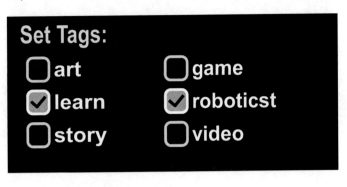

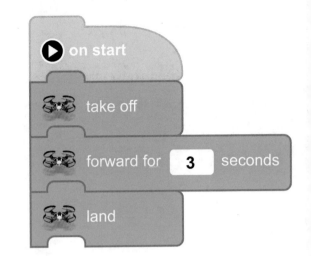

14) Click the **Save** button

You will see your project listed in the **My Projects** window.

15) Click on your project **Fly Forward and Save**. This will open your project back up.

16) Your Project has been saved. Make sure your drone is connected.

17) Click the play button to watch your code in action.

Terminology Block Review

In this lesson we used the **take off, forward,** and **land.** In the drone flight the real term for these blocks is different.

      * **take off** and **land = Throttle**
      * **forward** and **backward = Pitch**

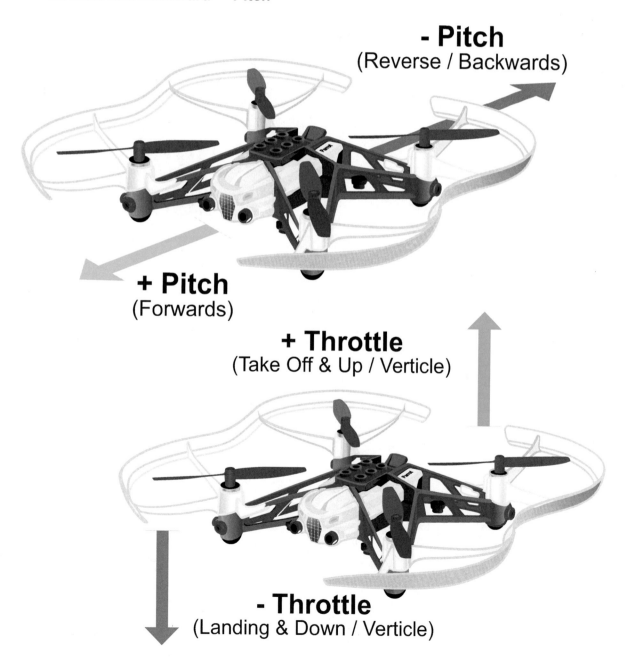

- Pitch
(Reverse / Backwards)

+ Pitch
(Forwards)

+ Throttle
(Take Off & Up / Verticle)

- Throttle
(Landing & Down / Verticle)

Lesson 3
Challenges

Challenge 1: Fly and Stop

1) Create a New Project with the blocks on the right.

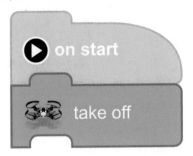

2) Between the **take off** and **land** blocks, insert a
   forward for [2] seconds followed by **stop** block.

3) Repeat step 2 three more times before you land.

4) The drone should take off, fly forward, stop, fly forward,
   stop, fly forward, stop, and land.

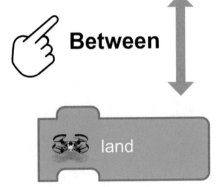

Think about it?

Did you successfully build the code? Try other combinations using the four blocks you've encountered. **take off, forward, stop,** and **land**.

Did you come up with any cool ideas? Make it a competition with friends and other drone coders. Get a group of drone coders and assign a task or destination. Using a start and stop watch, time each other to see who can do the task the fastest.

Challenge 2: Jumping Drone

1) For this challenge, find two or more block looking objects.

2) Place them both on the ground with a foot in between them.

3) Create the code that tells the drone to take off and fly over the 1st object and land. Continue to fly up and over the next object and land again. Repeat the process until you have no more objects to fly (jump) over.

Hint: Try using the **stop** block

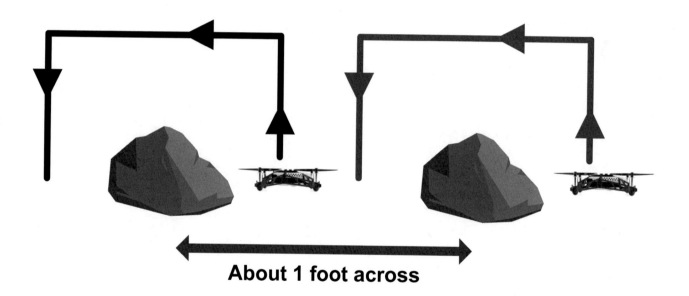

About 1 foot across

Think about it?

Were you successful? How would this apply to the professional world? What companies are using drones? How are they using drones? Do some research on the Internet to find out how companies are using drones in the professional world.

Challenge 3: Create your own combination

If you are feeling adventurous and want to try something new then try this challenge. Warning: We will be introducing a new block in this challenge.

"Stop" stops the Parrot drone from moving and puts it into a hover state.

"Wait" block waits for the specified number of seconds before continuing the script.

1) Repeat Challenge 2.

2) When you land, swap the **stop** block with the **wait** block.

3) Set the wait number to **4** seconds.

Think about it?

What did you learn? How does the **wait** block differ from the **stop** block.
Switch up the blocks. Have the drone fly **forward** and then **stop** and **land**. For the second pass, have the drone **take off, stop, fly forward, wait [2] seconds,** then **land**.

Were there any differences between the **stop** and **wait** blocks ability?

Lesson 4: Fly forward, turn around, and come back

We are introducing new blocks again.

Parameters:

<u>Angle</u>: number of degrees to turn clockwise

"Turn Clockwise" turns the Parrot drone clockwise at the specified angle.

turn left by **180** degrees

"Turn Counter-Clockwise" turns the Parrot drone counter-clockwise at the specified angle.

1) Create a New Project

2) Drag and snap a **take off** block.

3) Drag and snap a **forward for [3] seconds** block under the **take off** block.

4) In the **Library**, Drag and snap either a **turn left** or **turn right by [180] degrees** block under the forward block.

Take your finger, press, and hold on the **90°** degrees. This will open a pop-up window where you can change the turn angle.

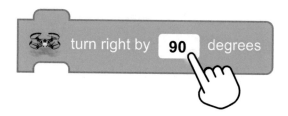

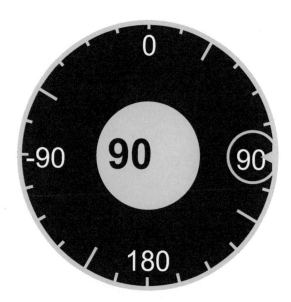

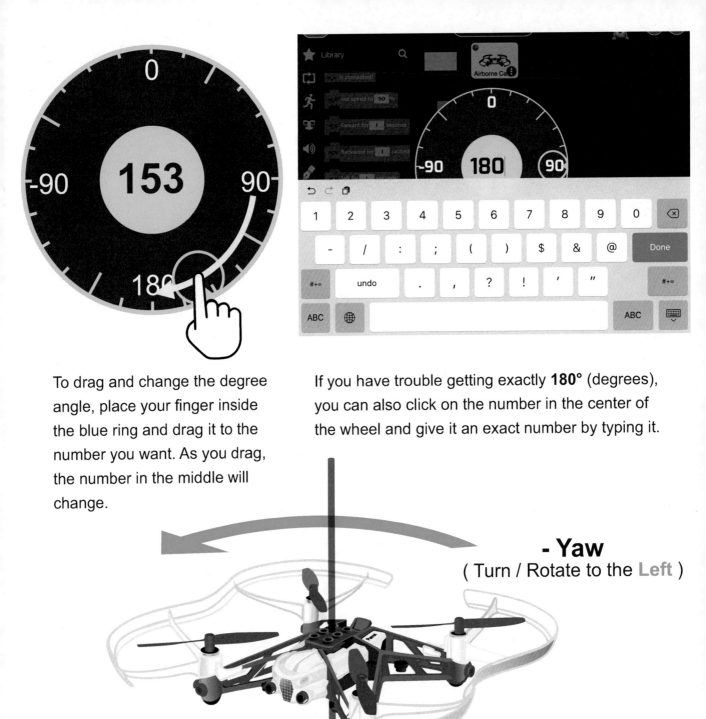

To drag and change the degree angle, place your finger inside the blue ring and drag it to the number you want. As you drag, the number in the middle will change.

If you have trouble getting exactly **180°** (degrees), you can also click on the number in the center of the wheel and give it an exact number by typing it.

- Yaw
(Turn / Rotate to the Left)

+ Yaw
(Turn / Rotate to the Right)

5) Drag and snap a **forward for [3] seconds** block under the **turn** block.

6) Drag and snap a **land** block under the **forward** block.

7) Save the project as **Fly forward, turn around, and come back**.

8) Press the play button to test your code.

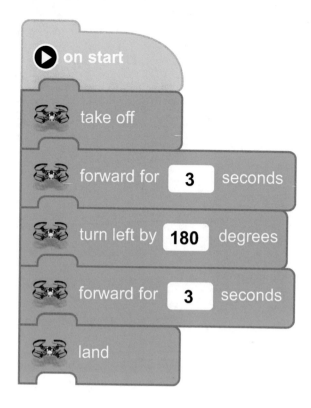

Lesson 4
Challenges

Challenge 1: 3 to 1

For all Lesson 4 Challenges you will look at a design and attempt to reconstruct it using the code blocks you've used so far. That includes the code blocks you learned in the challenges. Look at the image below. Your goal is to take off, fly forward and pause three times, turn around, and fly back to your take off position.

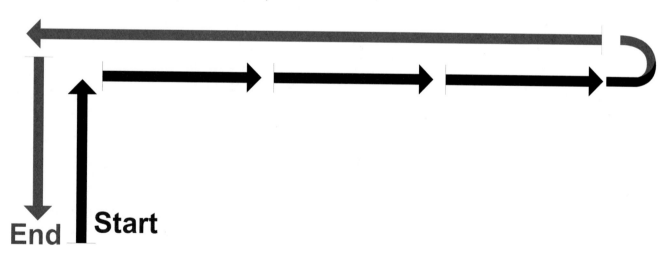

Think about it?

The challenges are starting to become a little harder but you can also do more now. Were you able to complete the challenge? Did we use any math in this challenge, and if so, what type?

Challenge 2: Fly, Wait, Land, Turn

Just like the last challenge look at the picture below. The picture below assumes you know how to take off and land. The **helipads** are spots where you must stop, land, and wait for at least 2 seconds before continuing.

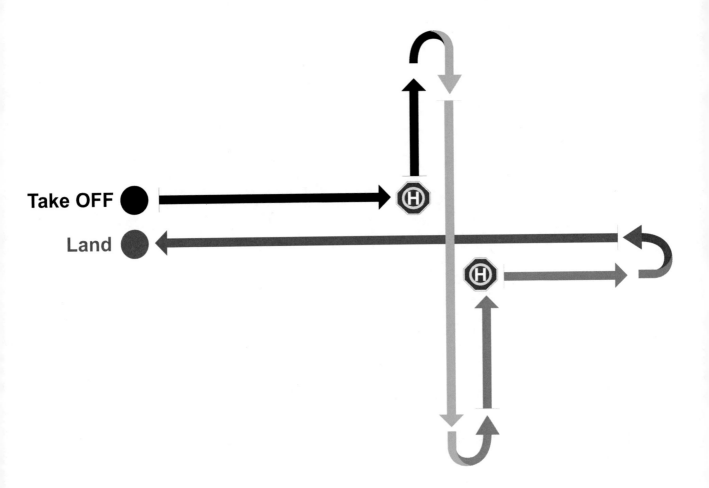

Think about it?

This challenge is a little harder than any other but it uses all the blocks we've learned so far. Did you get it to work? What does the image remind you of? Maybe a delivery system? Coding a drone is fun but always think of how you can use this in the professional world. Drone delivery is becoming popular around the world. Companies like Amazon are preparing for a full industry of drone delivery.

Challenge 3: Unique Shapes

Below are a few shape patterns that you might want to try if you'd like a harder challenge. Just like challenge 2: **helipad = stop, land,** and **wait for [...] seconds**. You define the number of seconds.

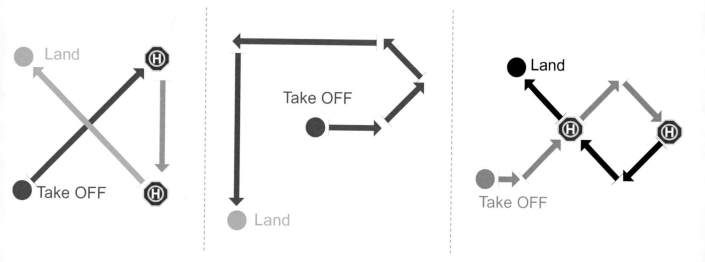

Think about it?

If you have the Airborne or Mambo, create your own custom drone delivery route. Have the drone take off from position "A" and fly to position "B". Pick up a package or Lego. Then fly to position "C" and drop off the package from "B". Then fly back to position "A". - If you have a delivery system, sometimes you will have to drive to one location, pick up a package, drop it off at a third location, and then drive all the way back to the first location. But with a drone you don't have to drive the long distance back, instead you can fly back to the original location saving time and money!

Lesson 5: Slide to the left, slide to the right

We are introducing new blocks again.

"Left For" moves the Parrot drone left for the specified number of seconds

"Right For" moves the Parrot drone right for the specified number of seconds

Think of the **left/right** blocks as tilting or leaning. If you are facing forward and lean to your right, your body might fall to right. It isn't turning, it is moving side to side. Take a look at the image below. In Drone Terminology, instead of **left** or **right** we use the term **Roll**.

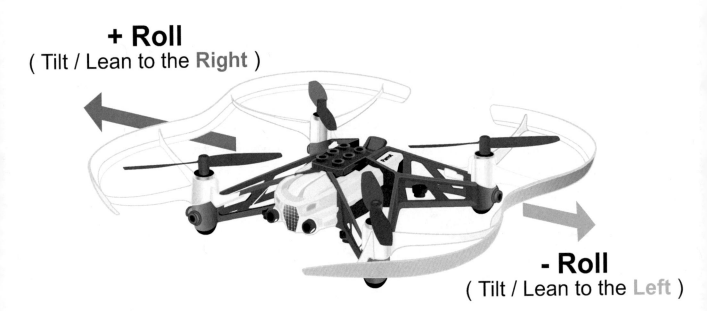

+ Roll
(Tilt / Lean to the Right)

- Roll
(Tilt / Lean to the Left)

1) Create a New Project

2) Drag and snap in an **on start** block

3) From the Library, drag and snap in a
   left for [3] seconds block.

4) Drag and snap in a **stop** block.

5) From the Library, drag and snap in a
   right for [3] seconds block.

6) Drag and snap in a **land** block.

7) Save your project as: **Slide to the left, slide to the right**.

8) Press play to test your code.

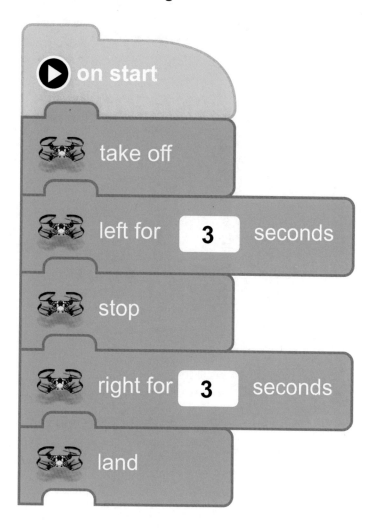

Lesson 5
Challenges

Challenge 1: Dodging Objects

Imagine you are in a city with tall buildings and you aren't allowed to fly over the building. Your only option is to **roll right** or **roll left**. Remember, the **helipads** are required landing zones for pickup. You must land and wait a minimum of 2 seconds before taking off to your next destination.

Complete the image below.

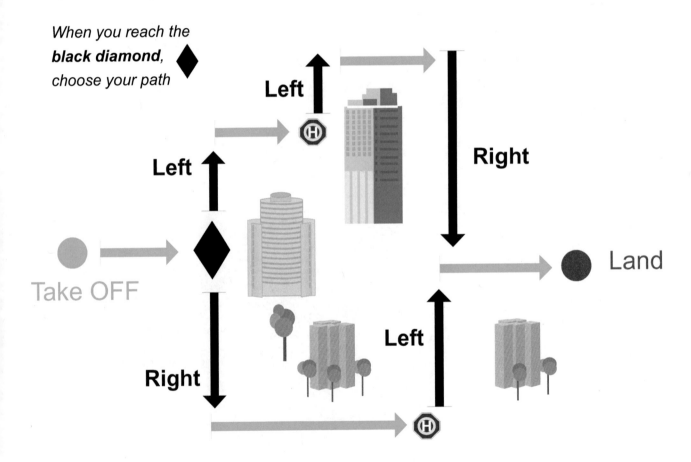

Think about it?

Which direction did you take? Left or Right? Did you remember to use the **right** and **left** blocks to roll (dodge) instead of turning? Did you land and wait on the helipads? Which distance was a longer route?

<u>Challenge 2: Roll and Pitch</u>

Terminology Time: Remember that...

    * **Roll** means move to the right or left.

    * **Pitch** means to move forward or backwards.

For this challenge try using the following block combinations when moving around objects.

*Weave in and out of the cones
while still flying forward!*

Think about it?

Did you get it? It's OK if you struggled. Note...at the time of this release, Tynker did not program in a block that automatically starts flying forward or backward (Pitch) without setting the number of seconds.

Lesson 6: The Repeat Block (Loops)

We are introducing new blocks again.

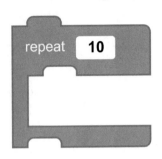

"Repeat" block repeats the script inside the specified <u>number</u> of times.

In this lesson we will be using the **Pitch** (move **forward**) and **Yaw** (turn **right by**) functionality.

1) Create a New Project

2) Drag and snap in a **take off** block

3) In the **Control/Flow** category, scroll-down until the color changes from yellow to orange and find the **repeat** block.

4) Drag and snap this block under the **take off** block.

5) Click on the **repeat** block number. Change the number **10** to **4**

6) Inside the **repeat** block, drag and snap in a **stop** block.

7) Inside the **repeat** block and under the **stop** block, drag and snap in a **forward for [2] seconds** block.

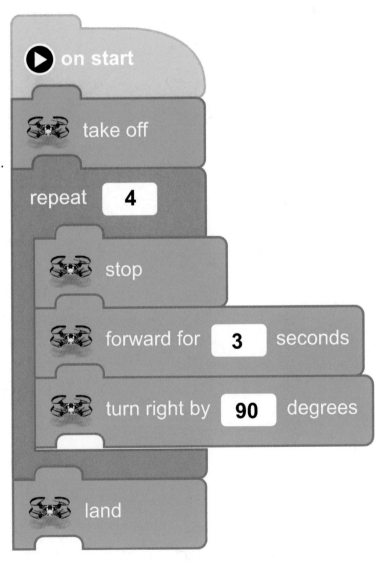

48

8) Inside the **repeat** block, drag and snap in a **turn right by [90] degrees**

9) Under the **repeat** block, drag and snap on a **land** block.

10) Save the project as: **Repeat - Fly in a Square**

11) Press the **Play** button and test your code. The drone should fly in a square.

Lesson 6
Challenges

Challenge 1: Make an 8

This challenge should be pretty obvious. Just like the lesson, duplicate the functionality so the drone flies in a number 8 path. It can be a boxed 8. Mimic the picture below. -- Advanced option: Make the drone fly forward, then backwards to create an 8.

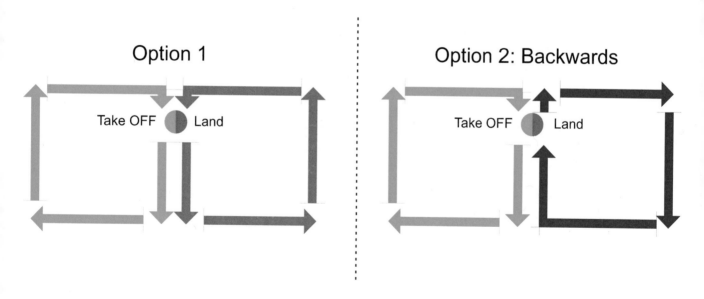

Think about it?

Which option did you choose? Did you do something different? Did you do both? Was it easy or hard? Are you starting to understand how the repeat block works?

Challenge 2: Fly in a Circle

OK, so flying in an 8 pattern is cool, but we want our drone to smoothly fly in a circle. For this challenge we will use new blocks:

"Start Rotating Left" starts the Parrot drone rotating counter-clockwise. The drone continues rotating until it receives a "Stop", a "Start Rotating Right", a "Rotate Right", or an "Emergency" command.

"Start Rotating Right" starts the Parrot drone rotating clockwise. The drone continues rotating until it receives a "Stop", a "Start Rotating Right", a "Rotate Right", or an "Emergency" command.

Use "Set Speed" to set Parrot drone to the specified speed.

Note: For this challenge you will need two of the blocks above and a **forward** or a **backward** block.

You will have to figure out the correct order, speed percentage, and number of seconds needed to fly in a full circle.

1) Create a New Project and Choose the direction you want to fly your circle: Left or Right.

2) Before using a repeat block, you must build the code for your drone to successfully fly in a full 360 degree circle without stopping.

3) Once your drone flies in full 360 degree circle, place the blocks inside a repeat block and make the drone fly at least 3 circles before landing.

Think about it?

Did you successfully fly in a circle using three blocks? What order did you place the blocks in? How many seconds did you use for each block? How many times did you fly in a circle.

Challenge 3: NASCAR Track

You should now know how to fly a full circle. The last challenge is for you to use a repeat block and fly the path around a NASCAR track. Use the image below as a reference.

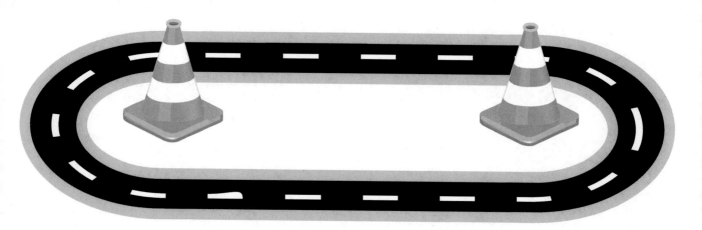

Think about it?

Was it easier or harder to code than creating a full circle? Did you build it successfully or were there any additional challenges? Were you able to make it fly without stopping? Be proud if you could make it fly without stopping, we couldn't.

Lesson 7: Variables

Understanding Variables

If you haven't figured it out yet, a **parameter** is the white space on a code block. It lets us input any value we want. So far, we've only used numbers. In the **forward for [1] seconds** block. The number **1** is the **parameter.**

OK, so now we understand what a **parameter** is. But what is a **variable**?

1) Create a New Project using the following blocks.

2) Save the project as:
Variables - Change once, update everywhere

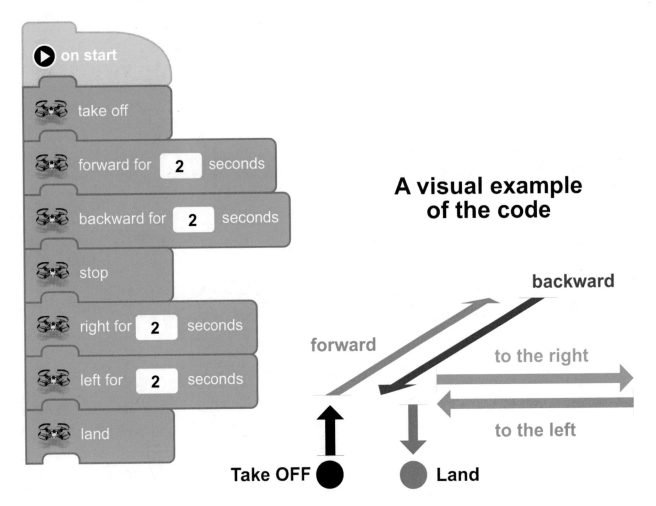

A visual example of the code

If we look at the blocks we can see that there are duplicates of the number **2**.
Now if we wanted to make the drone fly a longer distance in each direction we would have to change each number. That's too much work for a coder like yourself. Let's make it easier.

3) In the **Functions** category find the **+ New Variable** button and click on it.

4) A pop-up window appears called **Create a Variable**.
Name the variable: **lowestNum** or **min**.
(DO NOT check global)

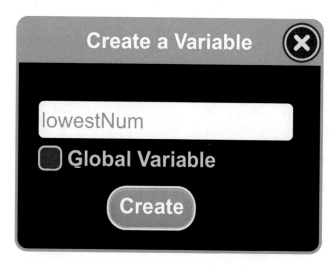

Note: programmers like to shorten words when coding. Num is short for number.

5) Click the **Create** button.

6) Notice in the **Functions** category, a block appears with the name you gave it. For this example we used **lowestNum**.

7) Now in the **Functions** category, drag and snap in the **set [select variable] to [0]** under the **on start** block.

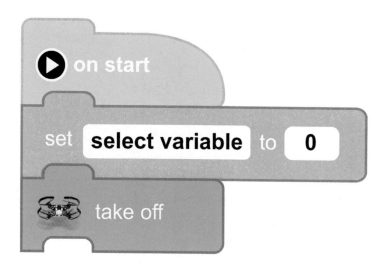

8) From the **Functions** category, drag and snap in your variable block over the **[select variable]** parameter and change the

9) Click on the **[0]** parameter and change it to **[2]**.

10) From the **Functions** category, drag and snap the **lowestNum** variable over all the the blocks with the **parameter** set to the number **2**.

11) Press the play button to test your code.

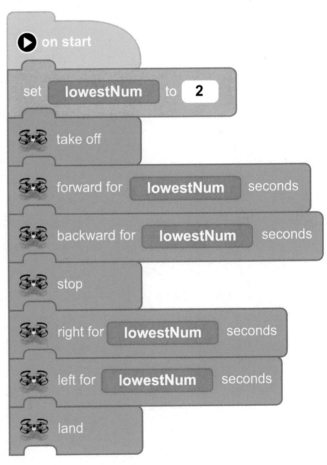

Think about it?

Try changing the number **2** to something else like **3** or **4.5** and test it out. This is one way a variable can be used.

Lesson 7
Challenges

Challenge 1: Step it up

For this challenge we will use new blocks:

"Up For" moves the Parrot drone upwards for the specified number of seconds.

View the image below. The goal is to use one to two variables and a repeat block to complete the task.

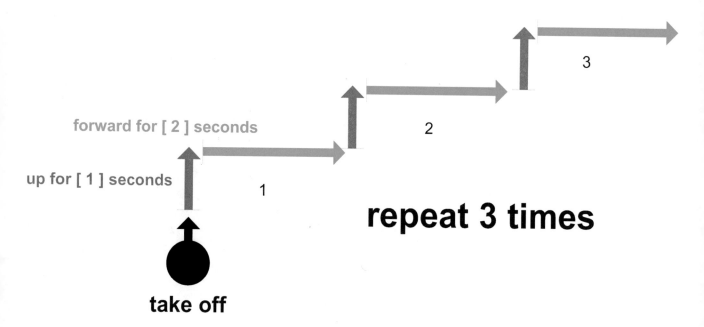

Think about it?

Were you able to complete the challenge? Did you use one or two variables? If you are in a group discuss how you completed the challenge. If you used only one variable be proud and explain it to your group. -- Note: to use one variable you will need to use a math block.

Challenge 2: Make a Table

For this challenge we will use new blocks from the **Math** category:

 " + " returns the addition of the two parameters

 " - " returns the subtraction of the two parameters

In this challenge you can only create a single variable. It is recommended that you set the value equal to the number 1. Use the Addition and Subtraction blocks with the variable to add subtract. Your goal is to match the image and fly in a box/cube. All blocks with parameters must contain the variable.

Hint: You may not need the subtraction block. Try adding the variable plus a number

Repeat 4 times to make 4 sides of the table.

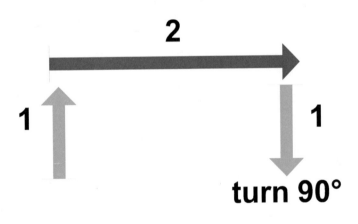

table example

Think about it?

Were you able to complete the challenge? This challenge takes it up a step because you can only use one variable. You have to figure out how to use the variables with all parameter blocks. -- If you get stuck, try to just do the first part without turning.
-- Don't give up!

Challenge 3: Random Values

For this challenge we will use new blocks from the **Math** category:

```
pick random   1   to   10
```

"Pick Random" returns a random number between the two parameters.

For this challenge you can either fly in a circle or fly in a box. You must create a single variable called: **size** and set it to the number **1** by default after the **on start** block.
Use the **set [select variable] to [0]** block.

Inside the **repeat** block add another **set [select variable] to [0]** block and replace the **[select variable]** with the variable **size**. Replace the parameter **[0]** with the **pick random** block. Set the first parameter equal to the number **1** and the second number equal to the number **3**. This will re-assign the value of **size** to either 1, 2, or 3 each time the loop runs.

The loop must run at least two times.

If you want to have a little more fun with random numbers, replace the **repeat** block **parameter** with the **pick random** block and set the values to **1** and **3**.

Think about it?

Did you like the random number generator? Were you amazed that you could re-assign a new value to the variable again? In Challenge 2, we incremented the value and returned the increment but the value stayed the same. In this challenge we changed the original value and made it new multiple times within the repeat block. It's a lot to take in for your first time, but just keep creating new code like this and it will start feeling normal.

Lesson 8: Functions

This will be our last chapter in this book. Once you understand functions you can do almost anything.

Understanding Functions

In Lesson 7 we learned about variables. **Variables** are blocks that can hold any type of value. You will be surprised to know that **functions** can have **functions** within them.

A **function** is a custom block like a **variable** that holds other blocks. It lets us use a group of code blocks multiple times.

Now you might be thinking of the **repeat** block. If you are that's good. The repeat block is a function, we just can't see how it works. But don't worry about that.

For now, let's build a **function** so we can start making the most awesome programs.

1) Create a New Project

2) Below is Lesson 4 Challenge 2

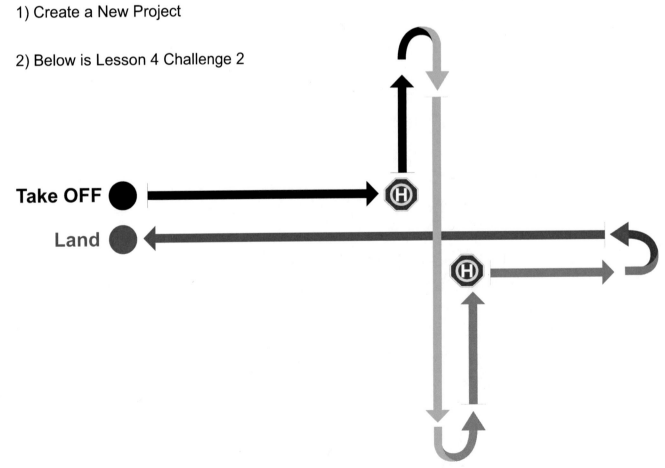

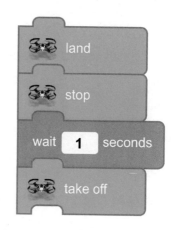

3) In this challenge we had to land and wait on each helipad for a minimum of 2 seconds.

4) Your code for landing may have looked like this...

5) For the challenge, you had to duplicate this code twice.

6) Using **functions** we can assign these blocks to the new function called: **reCharge**.

7) In the **Functions** category find the **+ New Function** button and click it.

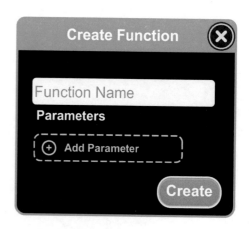

8) Just like the variable, a pop-up window will show called: **Create Function**

9) Set the Function Name to: **reCharge** and click the **Create** button.

10) A purple block will appear on the stage with your function's name.

11) Take the helipad code and snap it under the **reCharge** function block.

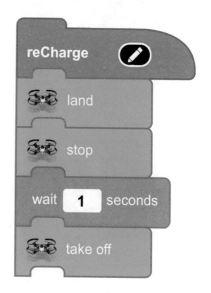

12) Your function now exists. Look in the **Functions** category towards the top. You should see two new blocks, both called: **reCharge**.

13) OK, using simple logic, let's fly in a box. We will use a loop and at every corner before we turn and take off we need to **reCharge**. This is visual example of the code inside the loop.

14) Here is what the loop will look like if it is run 4 times.

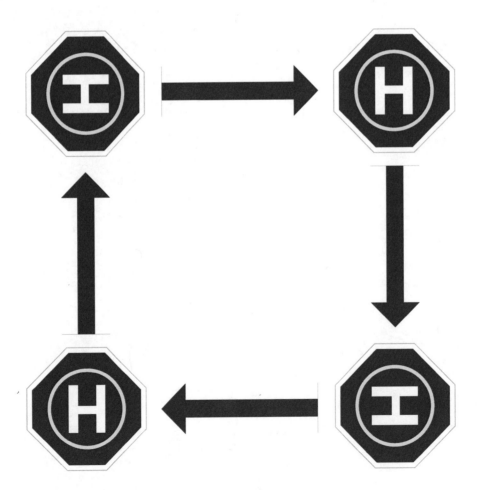

15) Here is the full code with the **repeat** block and **reCharge** function inside.

16) The moment we step into the **repeat** block the drone flies forward 1 second, and then it runs the **reCharge** function which entails (stop, land, wait 4 seconds, take off), the drone then turns right by 90 degrees, and the process repeats 3 more times and lands.

17) We used a function to convert 4 blocks into 1 block.

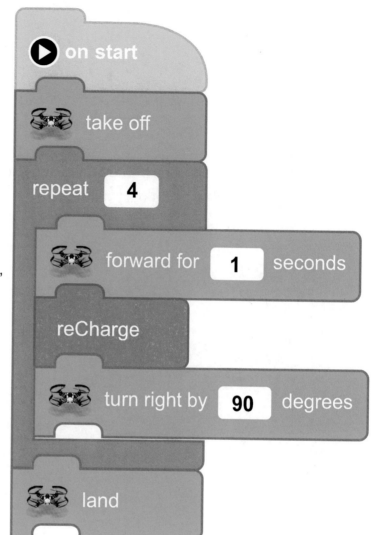

Think about it?

This was a very basic example but an important one. You now understand that you can shrink multiple blocks into one function and reuse the function over and over saving time. What else could you do with functions... Try out the challenges...

Lesson 8
Challenges

Challenge 1: Functions with Parameters

If you haven't guessed yet by the title, you can add parameters to your function. Let's bring up Lesson 8's function with code.

When we created the function **reCharge** the pop-up window had the option to add a parameter.

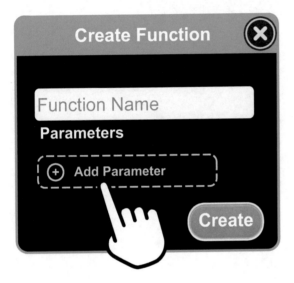

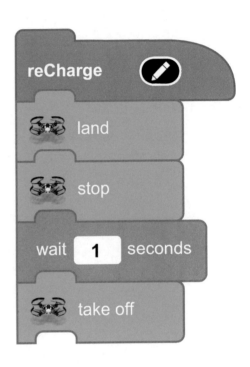

1) Open Lesson 8.

2) Locate the **reCharge** function block. Find the white pencil surrounded by the black oval (pill). Click on it. This will open a similar window to the **Create Function** called **Edit Function**.

3) In the **Edit Function** window you can add or remove parameters from the function.

4) In this challenge, click on the **+ Add Parameter** button.

5) Name the new parameter: **waitNumSec**.
  - This is that word shortening again.
  waitNumSec = Wait a certain number of seconds.

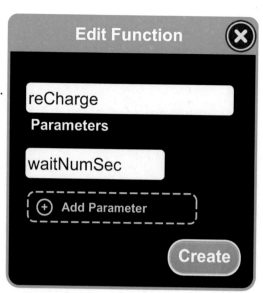

6) Click the **Save** button

7) Notice the function block changes and now has a prefilled custom variable called: waitNumSec

8) Place your finger on top of the new parameter variable: **waitNumSec**. Drag it down and over the number **4** in the **wait** block.

9) Your **reCharge** function should look similar to the code on the left.

10) To see the updated changes in the **reCharge** function block on the left, you need to switch to a different category and then back to the Functions.

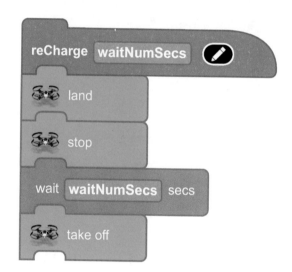

11) Your blocks on the left side should now be updated.

12) Continue onto next page for the challenge...

13) The challenge is simple.
The code on the right is the old block of code.

14) Create a new variable called: **num_4**

15) Under the **on start** block set the **num_4** variable to the number **4**.

16) Replace the old **reCharge** function block with the updated version.

17) Set the parameters for the **repeat** block and **reCharge** block to **num_4**.

18) Save project as:
Functions with Parameters

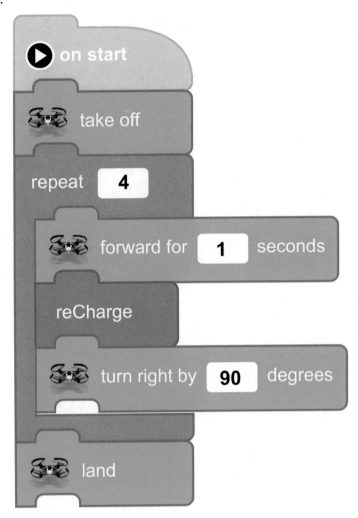

Think about it?

What did you think about this project? Are you starting to understand functions better? In the next challenge we will add more than one parameter to a function.

Challenge 2: Multiple Parameters

For this challenge we will use new blocks:

" = " returns true if the first value is equal to the second value and false otherwise.

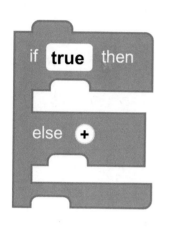

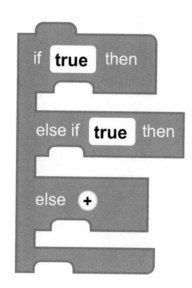

"If Else" Flow block runs the code inside the "if" if the parameter is true and the code inside the "else" if the parameter is false (but not both)
-- *Tynker*

If the 1st value is true then do it,
If the 1st value is false, then go to the next if. (else if)
If nothing is true, run else code.
-- *Ryan Jones*

1) Create a New Project

2) ReCreate the **reCharge** function from the last challenge with the parameter **waitNumSecs**.

3) Create a New Function called: **randomFlight** with a single parameter called: **number**

4) Drag and snap in an **if else** block under **randomFlight**.

5) Click the plus sign next to **else** so there are three options.

6) Using the **Math** blocks.
   Set the **if** parameter to: **[number] = [0]**
   Set **if else** to **[number] = [1]**

7) Under the **if**, insert the block **left for [2] seconds**.
   Under the **else if**, insert the block **right for [2] seconds**.
   Under the **else**, insert the block **forward for [1.5] seconds**.

8) Create a New Function called: **randomPattern**. Give it 2 parameters. Name the parameters **randNum1** and **randNum2**.

9) Create two new variables: **num_1** and **num_2**.

10) Set the values of both **num_1** and **num_2** under the on start block.
    Set the value of **num_1 = pick random [0] to [2]**
    Set the value of **num_2 = pick random [1] to [4]**

11) Under function **randomPattern** attach a **repeat** block.
    Put **randNum2** in the **repeat** block parameter.

12) Inside the **repeat** block snap in the function **randomFlight**. For the **randomFlight** parameter, drag in the variable parameter **randNum2**.

13) Inside the **repeat** block and under the **randomFlight** function, drag and snap in the **reCharge** function. For the **reCharge** parameter, drag in the variable parameter **randNum1**.

14) Now under the **set [num_2]** block, snap in the **randomPattern** block.
    Set the parameter **randNum1** to **num_1**.
    Set the parameter **randNum2** to **num_2**.

15) After the **randomPattern** block, snap in a **land** block.

Think about it?

That was the last project. Was it hard or easy for you? If it was hard that is to be expected. We did a lot. If you couldn't figure it out, don't worry. On the next few pages we will break down the code for this challenge and show you how we built the code.

If you have any additional questions about the code blocks remember to use the help monster. You can also try visiting my free site at:

https://github.com/drjonesy/ParrotDrone_Airborne_CodingWithTynker

Challenge 2: Multiple Parameters (Help)

In this section we will explain Lesson 8 Challenge 2 by breaking it up into how we built each function.

Building the reCharge function

1) Take a look at the function on the right.

2) To build the **reCharge** block. We created a new function called **reCharge** and gave it one **parameter** named: waitNumSecs.

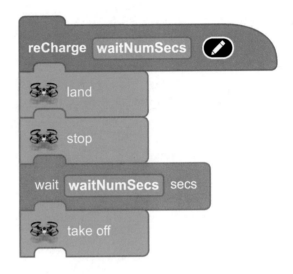

3) We then set the **wait** block parameter to the parameter variable **waitNumSecs**.

4) By doing this, when we use the the **reCharge** block and set the parameter to **4** or any other number, it assigns the **wait** block the parameter value of the **reCharge** block.

Building the randomFlight function

1) Take a look at the function on the next page.

2) This function is what might have made this challenge hard. This function uses two new blocks: the " = " block or **equal** block and **if, if else, else** block.

3) The " = " block compares two values. In our example we are comparing the **number** parameter variable to three possible answers.

4) The 1st test checks if **number = 0** and the 2nd test checks if **number = 1**.
- If the first two tests fail, then the last **else** block runs its code ignoring the first two test.

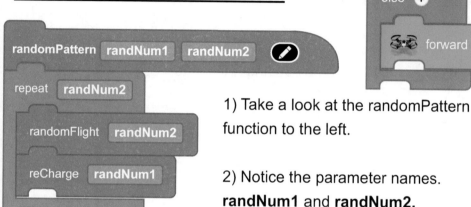

Building the randomPattern function

1) Take a look at the randomPattern function to the left.

2) Notice the parameter names. **randNum1** and **randNum2**.

3) All this function does is run a **repeat** block the number of times the value of **randNum2**. Within the **repeat** block it runs the function **randomFlight** and assigns the parameter variable **number** to the value of **randNum2**. Next, it runs the function **reCharge** and assigns the parameter variable **waitNumSecs** to the value of **randNum1**.

4) Finally, we use the **on start** block and set the values for the two variables we created: **num_1** is set to random number from **0** to **2** and **num_2** is set to random number from **1** to **4**. We then run the function **randomPattern** and assign the **randNum1** to **num_1** and **randNum2** to **num_2**.
Finish with a **land** block.

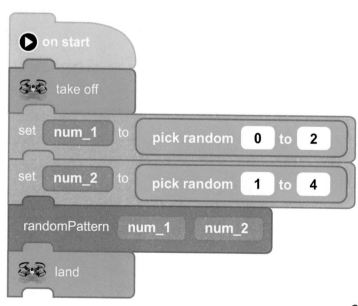

Resources and Notes

The resources currently available for this edition are listed below:

Hardware Needed:

- At the time of this release, the Tynker App for coding Parrot Mini-Drones would only work on Android and iOS tablets. They did NOT work on desktop computers or smart phones.
* You will need a tablet to code from (iOS or Android), must have bluetooth
* A Parrot Mini-Drone (Aerial and has bluetooth)

Websites Resources:

- github.com/drjonesy/ParrotDrone_Airborne_CodingWithTynker
- github.com/drjonesy
- ENVI-us.org/unmanned-aerial-vehicle
- Tynker.com
- parrot.com/us/

Notes:

-- While developing this course we tested all the drones and found that most of these examples run best on the Mambo or Airborne drones without the propellor shields (guards). You can still use the shields but you will likely have to adjust for air the resistance.

-- Beware of wind current. All these tests were done inside without any fans blowing against the drones.

Coming soon...

Code a Drone Using Blocks - Glossary
(refer to the github links in Website Resources for more info)

Ryan Jones is computer science engineer who loves knowledge and passing it on to others. He has a knack for simplifying complex terminology.

His passions include Tai Chi, Robotics, Sofware Development, the study of different cultures, language both spoken and programmed, new studies of science, and an unquenchable thirst for knowledge and understanding.

"No matter how old you are it's never too late to play with toys. Remember, the ones who develop and build the toys that you buy are adults."

- Ryan Jones

Revisions and Versions

2017 -

* Sept. 24   - Book Complete, Internal Review

                 - Version 1

* Sept. 26   - Reviewed with Norma Carter, a 4th and 5th grade teacher in Poway, CA

                 - Version 1: Published

* Oct. 8   - Updated Book Layout. See github for full revisions.

* Oct. 10   - © Copyright Revision by Dan Wolfson

Made in the USA
San Bernardino, CA
26 November 2017